The Global Flood of Noah

by **Bert Thompson, Ph.D.**

APOLOGETICS PRESS

Apologetics Press, Inc.
230 Landmark Drive
Montgomery, Alabama 36117-2752

Other Titles In This Series
The Bible Translation Controversy
The Christian and Medical Ethics
The Concept of Rational Belief
The Revelation of God in Nature
The Scientific Case for Creation

TABLE OF CONTENTS

CHAPTER ONE   Introduction 1

CHAPTER TWO   The Flood and Scripture 5
                    The Reason for the Flood   6
                    Supernatural Elements of the Flood 10

CHAPTER THREE   The Ubiquity of Flood Stories. 13

CHAPTER FOUR   Attacks Upon the Biblical
                    Doctrine of a Global Flood 17

CHAPTER FIVE   The Global Flood of Noah. 23
                    The Antediluvian World   24
                    The Need for an Ark   30
                    The Construction and Size
                        of the Ark   33
                    The Gathering, Storage, and
                        Care of the Animals   36
                    The Depth and Duration
                        of the Flood   41
                    The Testimony of the Apostle Peter 43
                    The Testimony of Jesus Christ   45
                    The Rainbow Covenant and Its
                        Implications   47

CHAPTER SIX   Conclusion 49

REFERENCES   55

DEDICATION

This book is dedicated to the memory of the late Ed Jones of Dalhart, Texas and his lovely wife Jane, who still lives there. This fine Christian couple has had an unwavering love for the Truth, and has provided generous assistance to those who teach it. That support is gratefully acknowledged by the author, and all those associated with the work of Apologetics Press.

1
INTRODUCTION

Name a subject, in religious circles, that has been scoffed at, laughed at, or ridiculed more than the account of Noah's Flood. Name a story that has been the brunt of more jokes, or has provided the unbeliever with more material with which to "poke fun" at the Bible, than Noah's ark. Likely it would be difficult to find any subject in our day and time which has received more derision, or been the subject of more mockery, than this story as recorded in Genesis 6-8.

There can be no doubt that the Genesis record of a global, universal Flood has become the target of sustained, concentrated attacks—the goal of which is to discredit, in its entirety, that account. Unbelievers of all stripes delight in attempting to undermine the faith of the believer by showing the "ridiculous nature" of the story as recorded in the book of Genesis. No doubt the reader has heard of "Dial-A-Prayer," where it is possible to dial a telephone number and hear a recorded message from the Bible. But have you heard of "Dial-An-Atheist"? Some time ago this writer was in western Tennessee, and was asked about such a phenomenon, which apparently was increasing in popularity. Upon listening to the recorded message, the listener was presented with a stern rebuke for believing in the God of the Bible. The atheist used as his "proof" of the non-existence of God the Flood story of Genesis 6-8, which he said no "enlightened, twentieth-century intellectual" would ever believe. He ranted and raved, listing as arguments against the literal nature of the Flood (and therefore the God behind the Flood) such things as the impossibility of gathering the animals into the boat, the size of the ark, the duration of the Flood, etc. Sadly, it is not just unbelievers who are attacking the Genesis account of the Flood. Some who claim to be religious have joined ranks with those unbelievers and are now quite vitriolic in their attacks on both the Flood and other related matters in the first eleven chapters of Genesis. As just one example of such (and these types of statements could be multiplied many times over), we cite the statements of authors Neal D. Buffaloe and N. Patrick Murray in their booklet, *Creationism and Evolution*:

> By contrast [to the historical view of Genesis—BT], the mainstream of Biblical scholarship rejects the literal historicity of the Genesis stories prior to Chapter 12, and finds the literature of parable and symbol in the early chapters of Genesis (1981, p. 5).

Later, in referring to the events of these chapters, the authors suggested that "these things never were..." (1981, p. 8). Indeed, the biblical account of Noah's Flood is being attacked, and those attacks are increasing both in number and intensity.

Whether or not the Genesis Flood has any significance at all depends on the answers to two important questions: (1) Was the Flood an actual event of history, or merely a myth or legend?; and (2) Was the Flood universal or just a local, Mesopotamian Flood? Additionally, one might inquire as to why a study of the Flood is important in the first place.

The subject of the Flood is a prominent story in the Bible, with more attention being given to it than even to Creation. Three of the first eleven chapters of Genesis are devoted to the record of the Great Flood. In fact, next to Creation, the Flood of Noah's day is the greatest single physical event in the history of the Earth—nothing comparable with it has happened since, nor will anything comparable happen again, until the final destruction of this Universe in the fiery judgment to come (II Peter 3). To use the words of professor Alfred M. Rehwinkel:

> The flood marks the end of a world of transcendent beauty, created by God as a perfect abode for man, and the beginning of a new world, a mere shadowy replica of its original glory. In all recorded history there is no other event except the Fall which has had such a revolutionary effect upon the topography and condition of this Earth and which has so profoundly affected human history and every phase of life as it now exists in its manifold forms in the world. No geologist, biologist, or student of history can afford to ignore this great catastrophe (1951, p. xv).

There are repeated references to the Flood account in many books of the Old Testament. In addition, Jesus and the New Testament writers often alluded to Noah and the Flood as if both had, in fact, existed (cf. Matthew 24:36-39; I Peter 3:18-22; Hebrews 11:7; II Peter 3:5-7). In previous centuries (as we will show in more detail later in this study), scientists and theologians attributed many of the Earth's features to the Great Flood, and generally were in agreement with the Bible's teachings on Creation and the Flood. Now, however, that is rarely the case. Furman Kearley has noted:

> *The World Book Encyclopedia,* for example, devotes four pages to glaciers and their effect on geographical formations; but it gives only a short paragraph on the Deluge and then only treats it as a story of the Bible, not as a historical fact. A certain textbook in physical science devotes thirty pages to the effect of water and glaciers in reshaping the Earth's surface, but it never mentions the Flood and any possible effects that it may have had (1979, p. 11).

Young people are being subjected to what may well represent one of the greatest challenges to their faith in recent years—the challenge of the conflict between evolutionary geology and the Word of God. It is utterly impossible to correlate the Bible with evolutionary geology (see Jackson, 1984, pp. 296-297), even though there have been some who have attempted such a compromise (e.g., Clayton, 1976; see also the refutation of such a position in Jackson and Thompson, 1992). As our children study under those who delight in ridiculing the Flood account, or who attempt to effect a compromise of evolutionary thinking and the biblical record, this challenge to their faith will become all the more real. In addressing this fact, Rehwinkel wrote:

> The shock received by the inexperienced young student is therefore overwhelming when he enters the classroom of such teachers and suddenly discovers to his great bewilderment that these men and women of acclaimed learning do not believe the views taught him in his early childhood days; and since the student sits at their feet day after day, it usually does not require a great deal of time until the foundation of his faith begins to crumble as stone upon stone is being removed from it by these unbelieving teachers. Only too often the results are disastrous. The young Christian becomes disturbed, confused, and bewildered. Social pressure and the weight of authority add to his difficulties. First he begins to doubt the infallibility of the Bible in matters of geology, but he will not stop there. Other difficulties arise, and before long skepticism and unbelief have taken the place of his childhood faith, and the saddest of all tragedies has happened. Once more a pious Christian youth has gained a glittering world of pseudo learning but has lost his own immortal soul (1951, p. xvii).

We must study this area, so that we, our children, and our grandchildren will be equipped to deal with these conflicts— because very likely they will occur. A careful study of the biblical account of the Flood can provide reasonable solutions for many of the difficulties that may arise, and that tend to cause doubt in the trustworthiness and reliability of the Bible.

2
THE FLOOD
IN SCRIPTURE

As we embark on this study of the Flood, and what the Bible has to say about it, let us state clearly that we do so from the perspective of a belief in the verbal, plenary inspiration of the Bible. We accept—though some modern "scholars" may be disgruntled with our approach—that God has given both **divine revelation** ("once for all delivered," Jude 3) and **historical fact** through inspiration. We stand firm on the fact that "every scripture is inspired, and is profitable for teaching, for reproof, for correction, for instruction which is in righteousness: that the man of God may be complete, furnished completely unto every good work" (II Timothy 3:16-17). We accept that "no prophecy of scripture is of private interpretation. For no prophecy ever came by the will of man: but men spake from God, being moved by the Holy Spirit" (II Peter 1:20-21).

We also firmly contend that a true exegesis of Scripture yields absolute Truth that is both ascertainable and knowable. We reject the concept now popular in some quarters that states: "I do not contend that it can be conclusively proven to 20th Century Americans that the Bible is inspired" (Clayton, 1976,

p. 89). Rather, we concur with Benjamin B. Warfield as he gave admirable expression to the concept of verbal, plenary inspiration of the Scriptures when he said:

> The Church has held from the beginning that the Bible is the Word of God in such a sense that its words, though written by men and bearing indelibly impressed upon them the marks of their human origin, were written, nevertheless, under such an influence of the Holy Ghost as to be also the words of God, the adequate expression of His mind and will. It has always recognized that this conception of co-authorship implies that the Spirit's superintendence extends to the choice of the words by the human authors (verbal inspiration), and preserves its product from everything inconsistent with a divine authorship...thus securing, among other things, that entire truthfulness which is everywhere presupposed in and asserted for Scripture by the Biblical writers (inerrancy) (1948, p. 173).

And so it is with the attitude which such reverence demands that we approach what the Scriptures have to say regarding one of the greatest of all physical events ever to have occurred on this Earth. As the prophet Isaiah wrote: "Come now, let us reason together..." (Isaiah 1:18).

The Reason for the Flood

According to the Bible, the world was created by God in six, literal 24-hour days. After the Creation (and the seventh-day rest), man was given three positive commands and one negative command. The three positive commands were: (1) be fruitful and multiply—fill the Earth (Genesis 1:28); (2) subdue the Earth and have dominion over it (Genesis 1:28); and (3) tend the garden of Eden (Genesis 2:15). The one negative command was to avoid eating the fruit of the "tree of the knowledge of good and evil" (Genesis 2:17). Every student of Bible history knows, of course, that the original human pair (Adam and Eve) transgressed the law of God and ate the fruit of the forbidden tree. For this sin, they were evicted from the garden paradise.

Outside the garden, Adam and Eve began to raise a family. [NOTE: According to Genesis 4:1ff., it was only **after** their eviction from the garden that any children were born, and since one of the original commands God gave them was to reproduce, they obviously weren't in the garden very long before they sinned.] The first two sons they named Cain and Abel. Cain murdered Abel, and eventually went into exile, separating himself from the main group of the family (Genesis 4:16ff.).

Like two distinct streams, the two family groups probably flowed along side-by-side for somewhat more than a thousand years. Eventually, however, the righteous began to marry indiscriminately, being motivated by lust. The Bible observes that "The sons of God saw the daughters of men that they were fair; and they took them wives of all that they chose" (Genesis 6:2). Out of these marriages came a generation of men and women who found themselves in total rebellion against God, as described in Genesis 6:5-7.

> And God saw that the wickedness of man was great in the earth and that every imagination of the thoughts of his heart was only evil continually. And it repented Jehovah that he had made man on the earth, and it grieved him at his heart. And Jehovah said, I will destroy man whom I have created from the face of the ground; both man, and beast, and creeping things, and birds of the heavens; for it repenteth me that I have made them.

That the righteous could lose their spiritual integrity by improperly motivated associations with the wicked should not shock us. Paul spoke of the evil consequences of such in I Corinthians 15:33 when he wrote, "Be not deceived: evil companionships corrupt good morals."

Before noting the result of God's wrath, perhaps it would be well to remember that we are not discussing just a "few short years" from the time of Creation to the events of the Flood. Sometimes we may discuss the accounts of the Creation, the subsequent fall, and the Great Flood so as to inadvertently leave the impression that they all three occurred within a very short span of time. The truth is, as Rehwinkel has observed in his book, *The Flood*, that the time from creation to the Flood was approximately 1,656 years (1951, pp. 24-25). That is a lengthy time span in human history. In that amount of time, people (especially people who lived to advanced ages as did the patriarchs) would have multiplied, and spread to many areas of the globe. Man was endowed with far greater vitality of body and mind than he is now (this is inferred, naturally, from the great ages to which he lived). Besides, there was a world of virgin soil, and unlimited, unused resources. Living longer under such conditions would also mean that man was much more prolific than he now is. Yet even in our age, when life spans are considerably shortened, 1,656 years would be enough time to produce an enormous population. During the century between 1830 and 1930, the world population doubled in number (i.e., it increased by about 850 million people within one century). Imagine—given the antediluvian setting of mild climates worldwide, great vitality, long life-spans, and virgin resources—the increase which would occur not in 100 years, but in **1,656 years**!

Some, of course, in an attempt to limit the Flood to a "local" event, have objected to the suggestion that mankind covered the globe. As one author stated:

> It would be highly unreasonable to suppose that mankind had so increased before the deluge as to have penetrated all the corners of the earth. It is indeed not probable that they had extended themselves beyond the limits of Syria and Mesopotamia (Hitchcock, 1854, p. 122).

The concept, however, that man must have been "limited" to the Mesopotamian region simply will not withstand the evidences at hand. In fact, it would be "highly unreasonable" to suggest—with the great ages of mankind in the antediluvian world, and the number of years involved—that man did **not** spread around the globe.

The stage was then set for God's wrath upon a sin-sick world. His decree was that He would destroy man, beast, and bird from the face of the Earth. There was, however, something (actually, some**one**) that prevented God from carrying out that decree immediately. It was the fact that a man named Noah, in the midst of sin all around him, had remained righteous. Noah was a good man. His character is described in Genesis 6:9 by three expressions. (1) "Noah was a just man" (i.e., honest—most likely an unusual trait for his day and time). (2) Noah is described as being "perfect in his generations" (i.e., upright). (3) Then the Bible adds that "Noah walked with God" (i.e., he was in fellowship, or had a personal relationship, with God).

Thus, a "probationary period" of 120 years was established by God (Genesis 6:3), during which Noah preached to the people of his generation (I Peter 3:18-20) and carried out the commands of God regarding the building of the ark (Genesis 6). After approximately 100 years, Noah's work was completed. Genesis 5:32 indicates that Noah was 500 years old prior to the events of Genesis 6-8; Genesis 7:6 indicates that Noah was 600 years old when he entered into the ark. It therefore appears from a straightforward reading of the text that Noah used 100 years or less of his probationary period.

For all his preaching, Noah's only "converts" appear to have been members of his own family group. It is important to observe that even though the converts were few to none, Noah did not change the message God had given him. We know this because the biblical account states that the ark floated. Had Noah altered God's commands, thereby disobeying Him, the ark surely would have sunk to the bottom of the sea. People must have grown accustomed to the large hulk of the great ark, and at the same time apathetic to Noah's message of salvation from impending doom. Sin continued as the probationary period drew to a close. The decree had been made; the grace of God had been extended. Now the time for action was at hand. Man's sin caused the Creator to send a worldwide Flood.

Supernatural Elements of the Flood

Before progressing to the factuality and universality of the Flood, let us note that we are speaking of three chapters of the Bible that entail the overruling power of an Almighty God in many miraculous events. And as a reminder let us also state, for emphasis, that we are dependent upon inspiration for exactly what **did** happen in the Flood. Critics of the Flood account have charged that, "If one wishes to retain a universal flood, it must be understood that a series of stupendous miracles is required. Further, one cannot beg off with pious statements that God can do anything" (Ramm, 1954, p. 165). Consistency, however, is not the norm for error, or those who defend it. The same Bernard Ramm who made the statement militating **against** miracles, also made the following statement arguing **for** miracles as an inherent part of the biblical system when he said: "The miracles are not warts or growths that may be shaved or cut off, leaving the main body of the gospel record untouched" (1953, p. 174). Which is it to be? Are we to allow for the miraculous or not? Apparently Dr. Ramm wishes it to be "yes" in regard to certain parts of the Bible, but "no" in regard to other parts.

What does Ramm mean when he says that "one cannot beg off with pious statements that God can do anything"? God **can** do anything consistent with His own nature. And He does not need Bernard Ramm, or others like him, to tell Him what He can or cannot do. God made it clear in these chapters that He was in control—from the bringing of the animals to Noah (Genesis 6:19-20) to the shutting of the door of the ark (Genesis 7:16). It was a miraculous situation from beginning to end. And though Ramm would disagree, to deny the operation of supernatural forces in the launching and control of the Flood is tantamount to denying inspiration. "The simple fact of the matter is that one cannot have any kind of a Genesis Flood without acknowledging the presence of supernatural powers" (Whitcomb and Morris, 1961, p. 76). Furthermore, even those who try to minimize the miraculous eventually end up returning to it. Ramm, for example, has admitted that the animals coming to Noah were "prompted by divine instinct" [i.e., a miracle—BT] (1954, p. 169).

The Genesis account makes it clear that God miraculously superintended the entire Flood process, and the Bible-believer who accepts verbal, plenary inspiration will not be the least bit embarrassed or ashamed to admit it. Ramm is right in at least one regard: the miracles are not "warts or growths that may be shaved or cut off, leaving the main body" of the record intact. John Whitcomb, in his classic work, *The World That Perished*, has listed at least six areas where supernaturalism is required in the Genesis Flood. Those areas are: (1) divinely-revealed design of the ark; (2) gathering and care of the animals; (3) uplift of oceanic waters from beneath; (4) release of waters from above; (5) formation of our present ocean basins; and (6) formation of our present continents and mountain ranges (1973, p. 19). There may be other areas where supernaturalism is present as well. One thing is for certain: **all** areas with which we have to deal in the account of the Flood cannot be accounted for by purely natural processes. However, we do not have to appeal to an "endless supplying of miracles to make a universal flood feasible" (Ramm, 1954, p. 167). As Whitcomb has noted:

> Apart from the specific miracles mentioned in the Scripture which were necessary to begin and to terminate this period of global judgment, the flood accomplished its work of destruction by purely natural processes that are capable of being studied to a certain extent in hydraulic laboratories and in local flood situations today (1973, p. 67).

Hence, the natural and supernatural phenomena worked side-by-side in the Flood. It did not require an "endless supplying of miracles."

3

THE UBIQUITY OF FLOOD STORIES

Professor Harold W. Clark, in his work, *Fossils, Flood and Fire*, has well stated:

> Preserved in the myths and legends of almost every people on the face of the globe is the memory of the great catastrophe. While myths may not have any scientific value, yet they are significant in indicating the fact that an impression was left in the minds of the races of mankind that could not be erased (1968, p. 15).

H.H. Bancroft noted: "There never was a myth without a meaning; ...there is not one of these stories, no matter how silly or absurd, which was not founded on fact" (undated).

The account of the Genesis Flood hardly stands alone. Researchers have described over 100 flood traditions from Europe, Asia, Australia, the East Indies, the Americas, East Africa, and many other places. Rehwinkel wrote:

> Traditions similar to this record are found among nearly all the nations and tribes of the human race. And this is as one would expect it to be. If that awful world catastrophe, as described in the Bible, actually happened, the existence of the Flood traditions among the widely separated and

primitive people is just what is to be expected. It is only natural that the memory of such an event was rehearsed in the ears of the children of the survivors again and again and possibly made the basis of some religious observances (1951, pp. 127-128).

Kearley has observed that "these traditions agree in too many vital points not to have originated from the same factual event" (1979, p. 11).

After the "trappings" are stripped away from the kernel of truth in the stories, there is almost complete agreement among practically all flood accounts: (a) a universal destruction by water of the human race and all other living things occurred; (b) an ark, or boat, was provided as the means of escape for some; and (c) a seed of mankind was provided to perpetuate the human race. These flood stories, of course, have aroused the interest of scholars, who have spent entire lifetimes studying, collecting, and cataloging them. In recent years, a collection of mythologies of all races has been published by the Archaeological Institute of America. The collection included flood traditions of many peoples as well. Johannes Riem, a German scholar, stated in the introduction to his book on the subject:

> Among all traditions there is none so general, so wide-spread on earth, and so apt to show what may develop from the same material according to the varying spiritual character of a people as the Flood tradition. Lengthy and thorough discussions with Dr. Kunike have convinced me of the evident correctness of his position that the fact of the Deluge is granted because at the basis of all myths, particularly nature myths, there is real fact, but that during a subsequent period the material was given its present mythical character and form (1925, pp. 7ff.).

Among the noted scholars of days gone by who have studied these matters in detail are such men as James G. Frazer (*Folklore in the Old Testament*) and William Wundt (*Elements of Folk Psychology*). Wundt, who did his utmost to find some kind of reasonable case for independent origins of the various flood sagas (and who had no great love for the biblical evidence), was forced to admit: "Of the combination of all these elements into a whole (the destruction of the earth by water, the rescue of a single man and seed of animals by means of a boat, etc.), however, we may say without hesitation, it could not have arisen twice independently" (1916, p. 392). Sir John William Dawson, the famous Canadian geologist, wrote:

> Further, we know now that the Deluge of Noah is not mere myth or fancy of primitive man or solely a doctrine of the Hebrew Scriptures. The record of the catastrophe is preserved in some of the oldest historical documents of several distinct races of men, and is indirectly corroborated by the whole tenor of the early history of most of the civilized races.
>
> As to the actual occurrence of the Deluge as a wide-spread catastrophe affecting, with a few stated exceptions, the whole human race, we have thus a concurrence of the testimony of ancient history and tradition, and of geological and archaeological evidence, as well as of the inspired records of the Hebrew and Christian revelation. Thus no historical event, ancient or modern, can be more firmly established as matter of fact than this (1895, pp. 4ff.).

It is to this "historical event" which is a "matter of fact" that we now turn our attention—the global, universal Flood of Noah.

4

ATTACKS UPON THE
BIBLICAL DOCTRINE OF
A GLOBAL FLOOD

As we launch an investigation into the factuality of the Genesis Flood, and its universal nature, it is entirely appropriate that we first mention some of the attacks that have been, and are being, made on the account of the Flood. In our introduction to this study, we made reference to the fact that atheists, humanists, and infidels of every stripe delight in ridiculing the story of the Genesis Flood. We also noted that even some who claim to be religious have now joined that attack. Such attacks from unbelievers are to be expected; the attacks by those claiming belief in and respect for God, however, come as something of a shock. Sadly, these attacks are becoming more frequent.

This has not always been the case. For centuries prior to our time, scientists and theologians alike attributed many of the Earth's features to the Great Flood of Noah, and were generally in agreement with the Bible's teachings on Creation and the Flood. As Harold W. Clark has observed:

The truth of the matter is that creationism is one of the oldest of all recorded explanations of the origin of the earth and its life. The book of Genesis was written a thousand years before the Ionian philosophers formulated their naturalistic cosmogonies. For over three thousand years it has been regarded as an authoritative statement regarding the beginning of the earth.... The period from the Reformation to the middle of the 19th century has been called the "Golden Age of Creationism." Many fundamental discoveries in science were made, and there was a genuine spirit of recognition of the validity of the Genesis story of creation and the Flood as a background for science. However, as geological knowledge grew rapidly in the 18th century, theologians found it increasingly difficult to adjust the new knowledge to the short chronology of Genesis. With increasing favor they began to turn to notions that were being propounded by scientists, not all of whom were sympathetic toward the Scriptural account of the past (1968, pp. 12,17-18).

Many of the greatest scientists of the past firmly believed in and accepted the biblical account of a global, universal Flood. Robert L. Whitelaw has noted: "Long before anyone knew of the carbon 14 clock and up until Darwin's day, the scientific world recognized the abundant evidence of a worldwide watery catastrophe such as the Genesis Flood" (1975, p. 41). Byron Nelson, in his classic text, *The Deluge Story in Stone*, called attention to this fact.

What is called "modern" geology has eclipsed Flood geology because of a dislike for those supernatural elements which are the backbone of Christianity. The Flood theory of geology has not been abandoned because it does not satisfy actual geological conditions. There is nothing known about the earth's geological state today which makes the Deluge theory any less satisfactory an explanation of the fossiliferous strata than in the days when the leading scholars of the world accepted it. Rather the contrary—there are facts known now about the geological conditions of the earth remarkably supporting the Flood theory which Williams, Catcott, Harris and others never dreamed of. **It is a disregard for God and the sacred**

record of his acts, and nothing else, which has caused the discard of the Flood theory to take place (1931, p. 137, emp. added).

Rehwinkel has addressed this point as well.

> Every student of the Bible and of geology knows there exists today a seemingly irreconcilable conflict between Genesis and geology. This conflict dates back about 125 years and had its origin in the rise of evolutionary geology. Up to that time, theologians and scientists were generally in agreement with the Biblical teachings concerning Creation and the Flood. But that is no longer the case. Today textbooks prescribed for courses in physical geography and geology in American high schools and colleges no longer teach a Biblical creation of the universe in six days of twenty-four hours each by a divine fiat. Some teachers, in fact, take delight in ridiculing the Biblical creation story and rule it out of modern thinking as naive, absurd, or as mere folklore of primitive people. Now and then there are still those who try to harmonize Genesis and the theories of geology by juggling language and extending the six days of creation into six periods of unlimited time, each measured by millions, or possibly billions, of years. Still others preserve an outward reverence for the Bible and speak of Genesis patronizingly as a beautiful but poetical conception of the origin of things (1951, pp. xvi-xvii).

These words cannot help but remind us of such statements as those by Buffaloe and Murray (quoted earlier) to the effect that the lessons of Genesis 1-11 are "the literature of parable and symbol." And authors such as these are not alone in their attempts to undermine belief in the literal, historical nature of the global Flood of Noah.

Religionists of both the past and the present have attacked, minimized, or tried to compromise the universal nature of the Flood. Among religionists of the past, Robert Jamieson, prominent nineteenth century Bible scholar, comes to mind. In the *Jamieson, Fausset and Brown Commentary* (1870), he presented a lengthy defense of the local flood theory. John Pye Smith, in his work, *The Relation Between the Holy Scriptures and Some Parts of Geological Science* (1854), strongly advocated a local flood. Edward Hitchcock, in his book, *The Religion of Geology and Its Connected Sciences* (1852), and Hugh Miller, in his work, *The Testimony of the Rocks* (1875), also defended the local flood theory, asserting that the biblical account of a global Flood simply was not acceptable.

In more recent times, Arthur C. Custance, the famous religionist/anthropologist, defended the local flood in his works, *The Extent of the Flood: Doorway Papers No. 41* (1958), and *The Flood: Local or Global?* (1979). John Warwick Montgomery, in *The Quest for Noah's Ark* (1972), joined Dr. Custance in defending the local flood theory. However, probably the most fervent, and best-known, advocate of the local flood theory in our day and time is Bernard Ramm, who attempted to refute the universal Flood in his controversial volume, *The Christian View of Science and Scripture* (1954). Ramm urged those of us who accept the biblical account of a global Flood to abandon our "hyperorthodox" attitude toward uniformitarianism and surrender the notion that the Flood was global/universal.

Apparently, Ramm is getting his wish—at least in some quarters. For example, John N. Clayton of South Bend, Indiana is on record as having stated:

> ...There is no way geologically of supporting the idea that there was a worldwide flood.... On the North American continent, for example, there is no place, no real conclusive evidence that there has ever been a flood over this continent.... You cannot go to geology and find evidence to support the idea of the worldwide flood.... **The Bible does not maintain positively that this was a worldwide flood.... It seems to me plausible that possibly the flood was confined to the known earth at that time** (Undated, emp. added).

Clayton has been joined in this kind of thinking by John Willis. In the commentary on Genesis which he authored, Dr. Willis wrote: "There is simply not enough concrete information to allow a dogmatic judgment in this matter." He then listed the various arguments set forth for a local flood, and ended with this assessment: "Geologists have discovered ample evidence of flooding all over the globe but no conclusive evidence of one universal flood. Rather, available remains can as easily point to local floods that occurred at different historical periods" (1979, p. 174).

Clyde Woods, in *The Living Way Commentary on the Old Testament: Genesis-Exodus*, apparently agrees with the assessment made by Clayton and Willis. He suggested:

> The extent of the flood has been disputed; some scholars insist that only a worldwide flood can satisfy the demands of the record, whereas others believe that the flood was limited to the area of man's habitation. **A local flood seems favored by the extra-Biblical evidence,** but it does appear at first glance that the more natural meaning of the text favors a universal flood (1972, p. 20, emp. added).

Woods then listed the various arguments for a local flood, and drew the following conclusion: "Thus, the local flood hypothesis seems to be a valid alternative."

Surely the careful reader will have noticed one very conspicuous and common trait of each of these statements. "You cannot go to geology...." "Geologists have discovered...no conclusive evidence." "A local flood seems favored by the extra-Biblical evidence." Notice how the conclusion preferring a local flood over the global Flood is based entirely on the so-called geological/scientific evidence, **without regard to what the Bible has to say!** This discussion, however, is about the **biblical** Flood. Does it not make sense, then, that we should go, first and foremost, to the Bible to see exactly what it has to say? As Byron Nelson so well stated: "It is a disregard for God and the sacred record of his acts, and nothing else, which has caused the discard of the Flood theory to take place" (1931, p. 137). It appears that there are some who "preserve an outward

reverence for the Bible," yet "speak of Genesis patronizingly."
Theodore Epp remarked concerning the local flood view:

> This concept seems to have gotten its greatest support from Christians attempting to harmonize the Bible with science. For the most part, the result has been a compromise between the Bible and historical geology, which is based on evolutionary thinking (1972, p. 138).

Sad, but true. And apparently this syndrome is becoming all the more common.

Since it is the **biblical** Flood about which we are speaking, and since it is from the Bible itself that we learn more about the Flood than from any other source, it is now to the Bible that we turn for information on whether the Flood was indeed a global event, or some minor, local "mini-catastrophe." The position presented here is that God's Word speaks plainly of a worldwide Flood. The evidences to that effect from both Scripture and science are overwhelming in nature and in number.

5

THE GLOBAL FLOOD
OF NOAH

As discussed earlier, whether or not the Genesis Flood has any significance depends on the answers to two important questions: (1) Was the Flood an actual event of history, or merely a myth or legend?; and (2) Was the Flood universal, or just a local, Mesopotamian flood limited to a small part of the then-known Earth? As Dawson put it:

> ...we have thus a concurrence of the testimony of ancient history and tradition, and of geological and archaeological evidence, as well as of the inspired records of the Hebrew and Christian revelation. Thus, no historical event, ancient or modern, can be more firmly established as matter of fact than this (1895, pp. 4ff.).

There is ample evidence to indicate some kind of flood occurred. The question is—was that flood local or universal? Men such as those quoted in the previous chapter would have us believe, for whatever reasons, that this flood was both local and limited. God's Word, however, states exactly the opposite. Let us examine the multitude of evidences from the Bible for a universal, global Flood.

The Antediluvian World
("The World That Then Was")

The Garden of Eden must have been a wonderful place in which to live—with an ideal climate and setting where man, the apex of God's creation, could exist in a covenant relationship with his Creator. The climate was apparently so mild that Adam and Eve could even exist on a day-to-day basis in the garden completely unclothed (Genesis 2:25). It was indeed a paradise setting. How long, however, did such a climate remain after man's fall, or did it continue at all outside the Garden of Eden? Several evidences, both scriptural and scientific, point to the fact that indeed, the mild climate present in the Garden did continue, at least for a while, and most likely even up to the time of the Flood.

In all likelihood, the antediluvian world was vastly different from the Earth of today. For example, we know from clear statements of Scripture (e.g., Psalm 104:8) that after the Flood God caused the mountains to rise, and the valleys to sink, evidently indicating that the mountains of the antediluvian world were not as high as those today. We also know from Scripture that on day two of creation, God "divided the waters which were under the firmament from the waters which were above the firmament" (Genesis 1:7). There was apparently, then, a water "canopy" of some kind above the Earth (the same canopy that would later shower rain on the Earth for 40 days and 40 nights—Genesis 7:17 and 8:6). What effect(s) would this canopy have on the Earth's climate if it did, in fact, exist? Whitcomb and Morris have suggested:

> The most immediate and obvious of these effects would be to cause a uniformly warm temperate climate around the earth. Such water vapor as is present in the atmosphere today has this specific effect of regulating the earth's temperature. The inferred antediluvian vapor envelope would have produced this result in much greater degree, with a larger percentage of the sun's incoming radiant energy being absorbed and retained and uniformly distrib-

uted over the earth than at present, both seasonally and latitudinally.... The constant battle of "fronts" would be mostly absent, so that antediluvian climates were not only warm but also without violent windstorms (1961, p. 240).

Various other writers (Rehwinkle, *The Flood*; Patten, *The Biblical Flood and the Ice Epoch*; et al.) have made reference to the possibility of an antediluvian world different from our own, but most have done so, correctly, in cautious tones, attempting to be careful so as to both respect Scripture and avoid forcing unwarranted conclusions. For example, Whitcomb and Morris have stated:

> Although we can as yet point to no definite scientific verification of this pristine vapor protective envelope around the earth, neither does there appear to be any inherent physical difficulty in the hypothesis of its existence, and it does suffice to explain a broad spectrum of phenomena both geological and Scriptural....
>
> We feel warranted, therefore, in suggesting such a thermal vapor blanket around the earth in pre-Pleistocene times as at least a plausible working hypothesis, which seems to offer satisfactory explanation of quite a number of Biblical references and geophysical phenomena. The detailed physics of this inferred antediluvian atmosphere is bound to be uncertain as yet, especially in view of the fact that so little is known about even the present atmosphere, but there seems to be no inherent physical difficulty with the concept (1961, pp. 241,256).

There have been those, however, who have taken exception to the canopy theory. For example, John N. Clayton has vociferously objected to it, and has raised what he considers to be a number of serious problems (1980, pp. 5-6). However, such arguments are indicative of a lack of study in this area. *The Genesis Flood* was published in 1961. Since then, much additional research has been done, and many of the objections to the canopy theory have been answered. For example, the reader interested in an examination of data bearing on a global water canopy may wish to refer to the classic text in this area, *The*

Waters Above, by Joseph Dillow (1981), or to technical research reports such as the one presented at the second International Conference on Creationism (see Rush and Vardiman, 1990, pp. 231-245). Interestingly, even evolutionists speak conclusively of a universally mild climate characterizing the Earth at one time. Speaking of the age of reptiles, for example, E.H. Colbert said:

> Many lines of dinosaurs evolved during the 100 million years or more [according to the evolutionists' timetable— BT] of Mesozoic history in which they lived.... In those days the earth had a tropical or sub-tropical climate over much of its land surface, and in the widespread tropical lands there was an abundance of lush vegetation. The land was low and there were no high mountains forming physical or climatic barriers (1949, p. 71).

W.J. Arkell, in summarizing the so-called Jurassic Era, remarked that "...a fairly rich flora of temperate facies flourished within or near both the Arctic and Antarctic Circles, in East Greenland and Grahamland" (1956, p. 615).

Much geological evidence does point, in fact, to a universally warm climate during the antediluvian era. The canopy theory harmonizes beautifully in many respects with this geological evidence. Such a canopy would likely give the Earth a "greenhouse" effect, producing a warm, uniform climate worldwide—due, in large part, to the trapping of the Sun's incoming radiant energy. This concept fits the picture given us by the flora and fauna of the past world. The naturalist Alfred Russel Wallace, a contemporary of Charles Darwin, commented:

> There is but one climate known to the ancient fossil world as revealed by the plants and animals entombed in the rocks, and the climate was a mantle of spring-like loveliness which seems to have prevailed continuously over the whole globe. Just how the world could have been this warm all over may be a matter of conjecture; that it was so warmed effectively and continuously is a matter of fact (1876, 1:277).

Samuel Kinns quotes a writer by the name of Figuier as stating almost the same thing:

> It is a remarkable circumstance that conditions of equable and warm climate, combined with humidity, do not seem to have been limited to any one part of the globe, but the temperature of the whole seems to have been nearly the same in very different latitudes. From the equatorial regions up to Melville Island, in the Arctic Ocean, where in our days eternal frost prevails—from Spitzbergen to the center of Africa, the Carboniferous flora is identically the same. When nearly the same plants are found in Greenland and Guinea; when the same species, now extinct, are met with of equal development at the equator as at the pole, we cannot but admit that at this period the temperature of the globe was nearly alike everywhere. What we now call climate was unknown in these geological times. There seems to have been then only one climate over the whole globe (Kinns, 1886, p. 166).

Fossils of plants and man-made tools show that the African desert was at one time covered with luxuriant vegetation and was inhabited by man. Similar remains have been discovered in the Gobi Desert of China and in other great desert areas throughout the world. The Arctic regions forcefully testify to the warm temperatures that apparently were once to be found there. The Arctic Islands, north of Siberia, are densely packed with the remains of elephants and other mammals, along with the dense tangles of fossil trees and other plants. The great coal beds at both poles speak of the warm conditions that must have prevailed at one time throughout the world. Whitcomb (quoting from *National Geographic*, February, 1963, pp. 288,296) has commented concerning the coal beds of Antarctica: "The frozen and forbidden shoreline of the South Polar continent challenges our imagination as to its former condition. The fact that it was once warm and humid and had abundant vegetation is shown by 'wide-spread discoveries of coal and petrified wood' " (1973, p. 82; see also *National Geographic*, November, 1971, p. 653). The stratified rocks of Antarctica have yielded fossils of such plants as ferns, oaks, magnolias, ginkos and breadfruits (the last mentioned usually growing only in India and South China). Many of the plants buried in the frozen strata can grow only in climates entirely different from those where their remains are found. Additionally, Whitcomb and Morris (and others) have called attention to the "large numbers of fossil mammals, apparently trapped and in some cases partially frozen before the soft parts had decayed" (1961, p. 288).

These facts, and others like them far too numerous to discuss here, tend to support the contention that "the world of Adam and his immediate descendants contained proportionately more habitable land than the world today. There were no enormous waste areas, such as the great deserts of Africa, Asia, America and Australia" (Rehwinkel, 1951, p. 2). Some creationist scientists have suggested the likelihood that the early Earth (i.e., prior to the Flood) may have been a singular land mass. If this were true, that would certainly account for more "habitable land" and, along with the pre-Flood canopy, help explain a globally equitable climate. While it is neither possible nor desirable to be dogmatic on these points, they do bear serious consideration.

As an aside, although we do not have the space here to develop the concept in its entirety, we might also mention that antediluvian longevity might also best be explained on the basis of something to do with the vapor canopy. Remember that "before the Flood, therefore, everything was conducive to physical health and longevity. Equable temperatures, freedom from environmental radiation, and other factors attributable to the vapor canopy all contributed to this effect" (Whitcomb and Morris, 1961, p. 404). The early chapters of Genesis record great life-spans for the patriarchs, topped by Methuselah at 969 years. This may seem incomprehensible to us, but obviously was quite possible under the conditions prevailing in the antediluvian world. Donald Patten and his son Phillip, in their unpublished manuscript, *The Longevity Accounts in Genesis, Job, Josephus, and Augustine*, have suggested that perhaps a much higher carbon dioxide content in the atmosphere would have slowed down maturation rates and induced longer life. Slowing maturation would also produce, in some instances, giantism. Geological and biblical evidences do indicate that plants, animals, and even some humans of the past were larger than we now seem to observe (e.g., grape clusters carried back from the land of Canaan by the twelve spies, dinosaurs, and Goliath, just to name a few). As one writer has stated:

> The Flood completely altered the climatic balance. The ozone layer was disturbed thereby letting a greater quantity of harmful ultra-violet radiation penetrate to the ground. The carbon dioxide balance was altered giving much reduced percentages. Thus life spans were dramatically shortened.... The curve of declining longevity is perfectly consistent with a gradual reduction of carbon dioxide. The average age of antediluvians, Enoch excepted, was 912, but this reduced in a mathematical curve after the Flood thereby suggesting a physical cause (Fisher, 1982, p. 54).

Indeed, only after the Flood do we begin to notice severe reductions in men's ages. The data do suggest a "physical cause." [Once again, however, in an effort to placate those who are intent on viewing mankind through evolutionary presuppositions, some have attempted to "explain away" the great ages of the patriarchs. For example, John N. Clayton has suggested that possibly the patriarchs did not live to these great ages, but rather had their ages calculated via calling the "years" by our "months," subsequently necessitating that the patriarchs vast ages be divided by a factor of twelve in order to ascertain the correct age (1978, pp. 11-13). Filby has dealt with this concept, and shown how ridiculous this assertion is. "This we reject completely, as not only can it be shown to be absolutely wrong, but it makes more difficulties than it solves. Enoch, we are told, had a son Methuselah when he was sixty-five. If we divide by twelve he had a son when he was 5.4 years old!" (1970, p. 101).

There is no reason to have to "explain away" the long ages of the patriarchs. They are to be accepted just as they are (see Thompson, 1992, 12:17-20).]

But questions naturally arise. What was the physical cause of the decrease in man's longevity? What was the cause of the dramatic environmental changes that have obviously occurred? What caused the two Poles of the Earth to become frozen wastelands when they were once beautiful landscapes? What caused otherwise lush tropical areas to be turned into vast deserts? **Something** obviously happened. That "something" could well have been the global Flood of Noah.

The Need for an Ark

According to the account recorded in Genesis 6-8, one hundred years before the Flood God chose to reveal to a single human being, Noah by name, His intent to destroy the Earth by water—because of man's rebellion. God instructed Noah to make the necessary preparations for this coming judgment by building an ark that would be the instrument for saving not only his own family, but also the seed of all air-breathing creatures in the world. Rehwinkle noted:

> The word "ark" seems to be derived from the Egyptian language and signifies "chest" or something to float. The word occurs only twice in the Bible, here for the ark of Noah and again in Ex. 2:3-5 for the ark of bulrushes in which the infant Moses was saved from the cruel decree of Pharaoh (1951, p. 58).

Before examining the construction and size of the Noah's ark, a more basic question obviously comes to mind: If the Flood were local, as some Bible critics maintain, **why would Noah have needed to build such an ark in the first place?** Whitcomb has remarked that:

> **...there would have been no need for an Ark at all if the flood was local in extent.** The whole procedure of constructing such a vessel, involving over 100 years of planning and toiling, simply to escape a local flood can hardly

be described as anything but utterly foolish and unnecessary! How much more sensible it would have been for God simply to have warned Noah of the coming destruction in plenty of time for him to move to an area that would not have been affected by the Flood, even as Lot was taken out of Sodom before the fire fell from heaven. Not only so, but also the great numbers of animals of all kinds, and certainly the birds, could easily have moved out of the danger zone also, without having to be stored in a barge for an entire year! The Biblical record simply cannot be harmonized with the concept of a flood that was confined to the Near East (1973, p. 47, emp. in orig.).

This is a point that almost all advocates of the local flood theory have missed, or purposely failed to discuss. In fact, Whitcomb and Morris have suggested: "The writers have had a difficult time finding local-Flood advocates that are willing to face the implications of this particular argument" (1961, p. 11). One can certainly understand why.

In a valiant, but doomed, effort to support the concept of a local flood, Custance suggested that the entire ark-building episode was merely an "object lesson" for the antediluvians. He wrote:

It would require real energy and faith to follow Noah's example and build other Arks, but it would have required neither of these to pack up a few things and migrate. There is nothing Noah could have done to stop them except disappearing very secretly. Such a departure could hardly act as the kind of warning that the deliberate construction of the Ark could have done. And the inspiration for this undertaking was given to Noah by leaving him in ignorance of the exact limits of the Flood. He was assured that all mankind would be destroyed, and probably supposed that the Flood would therefore be universal. This supposition may have been quite essential for him (1958, p. 18).

Whitcomb and Morris, in responding to this suggestion, asked:

But how can one read the Flood account of Genesis 6-8 with close attention and then arrive at the conclusion that the Ark was built **merely** to warn the ungodly, and not **mainly** to save the occupants of the Ark from death by drowning? And how can we exonerate God Himself from the charge of deception, if we say that He led Noah to believe that the Flood would be universal, in order to encourage him to work on the Ark, when He knew all the time that it would not be universal? (1961, p. 12, emp. in orig.).

Further, consider that Genesis 7:21-23 plainly states:

All flesh died that moved upon the earth, both birds, and cattle, and beasts, and every creeping thing that creepeth upon the earth, and every man: all in whose nostrils was the breath of life, of all that was on the dry ground, died. And every living thing was destroyed that was upon the face of the ground, both man, and cattle, and creeping things, and birds of the heavens; and they were destroyed from the earth.

Again, Whitcomb and Morris have observed:

These are exactly the same terms used in the first chapter of Genesis to describe the various kinds of land animals which God created.... The fact of the matter is that no clearer terms could have been employed by the author than those which he did employ to express the idea of **the totality of air-breathing animals in the world.** Once this point is conceded, all controversy as to the geographical extent of the Deluge must end; for no one would care to maintain that all land animals were confined to the Mesopotamian Valley in the days of Noah! (1961, p. 13, emp. in orig.).

One final point needs to be mentioned. Some today are fervent in their insistence that the ark has been found on top of the 17,000-foot-high Mt. Ararat in Turkey. Among that number is John Warwick Montgomery (1972). Montgomery, however, is a proponent of the local flood theory. How, we are forced to wonder, can a man claim to accept biblical and/or scientific evidence that he feels would point to the remains of Noah's ark being on the top of Mt. Ararat in Turkey, and then turn right around and deny **the biblical testimony to the global Flood that supposedly put it there?** Does Dr. Montgomery understand what he is asking us to believe? To claim that the remains of the ark are on top of the 17,000-foot-high Mt. Ararat, while at the same time insisting that it was put there by a **local flood,** is to strain at the gnat and swallow the camel. [NOTE: We do not accept Montgomery's claim that the ark can be proven to be on Ararat, but that is beyond the scope of this book. For a discussion of this point, see Major, 1994, 14:39.]

The Construction and Size of the Ark

God told Noah (Genesis 6:15) to make "the length of the ark three hundred cubits, the breadth of it fifty cubits, and the height of it thirty cubits." If we are to understand the size of the ark, we must first understand the length of the cubit. "The Babylonians had a 'royal' cubit of about 19.8 inches, the Egyptians had a longer and a shorter cubit of about 20.65 and 17.6 inches respectively, while the Hebrews apparently had a long cubit of 20.4 inches (Ezek. 40:5) and a common cubit of about 17.5 inches" (Whitcomb and Morris, 1961, p. 10). Rehwinkel has noted:

> It is generally supposed that the cubit is the distance from the point of the elbow to the tip of the middle finger. Translated into our own standard of measurements, the common cubit is estimated at about 18 inches. But Petrie, a noted Egyptologist, is of the opinion that it measured 22½ inches. Whether or not Noah's cubit was comparable to any one of the cubits now known to us, no one is able to determine. It is not unreasonable, however, to assume that, in keeping with nature about him, man before the Flood was more fully developed and was of larger stature than now and the length from his elbow to the tip of his finger was even longer than the suggested 22½ inches. Two feet may be more nearly correct.... But accepting the lower figures and placing the cubit at eighteen inches and then again at twenty-four inches, we get the following results: According to the lower standard, the ark would have measured 450 feet in length, seventy-five feet in width, and forty-five feet in height. According to the higher figure, the length would have been six hundred feet; the width, one hundred feet; the height, sixty feet....

The ships of the maritime nations of the world never approached the dimensions of the ark until about a half century ago (1951, pp. 59-60).

In fact, as Filby has pointed out, as late as 1858 "the largest vessel of her type in the world was the P&O liner *Himalaya*, 240 feet by 35 feet." It was in that year that Isambard K. Brunel produced

> ...the *Great Eastern*, 692 feet by 83 feet by 30 feet of approximately 19,000 tons...five times the tonnage of any ship then afloat.... Still more interesting are the figures for the *Great Britain*, designed by I.K. Brunel in 1844. Her dimensions were 322 feet by 51 feet by 32½ feet, so that the ratios are almost exactly those of the Ark. Brunel had the accumulated knowledge of generations of shipbuilders to draw upon. The Ark was the first of its kind! (1970, p. 93).

Using the conservative estimate of 17.5 inches for a cubit, Whitcomb and Morris have shown that the ark would have been 437.5 feet long, 72.92 feet wide, and 43.75 feet high. In its three decks (Genesis 6:16) it had a total deck area of approximately 95,700 square feet—the equivalent of slightly more than twenty standard basketball courts. Its total volume would have been 1,396,000 cubic feet. The gross tonnage (measurement of cubic space rather than weight, one ton being equivalent to 100 cubic feet of usable storage space) was about 13,960 tons (1961, p. 10).

Critics of the Flood account have often stated that the ark was not large enough to handle its assigned cargo. Such critics, however, generally have not taken the time to consider just how large the ark really was, or the cargo it had to carry. As Whitcomb has noted:

> For the sake of realism, imagine waiting at a railroad crossing while ten freight trains, each pulling 52 boxcars, move slowly by, one after another. That is how much space was available in the Ark, for its capacity was equivalent to 520 modern railroad stock cars. A barge of such gigantic size, with its thousands of built-in compartments (Gen. 6:14) would have been sufficiently large to carry two of

every **species** of air-breathing animal in the world today (and doubtless the tendency toward taxonomic splitting has produced more "species" than can be justified in terms of Genesis 'kinds') on only half of its available deck space. The remaining space would have been occupied by Noah's family, five additional representatives of each of the comparatively few kinds of animals acceptable for sacrifice, two each of the kinds that have become extinct since the Flood, and food for them all (Gen. 6:21) (1973, p. 23, emp. in orig.).

In *The Genesis Flood*, Whitcomb and Morris gave extensive investigation to the numbers of animals that would have been on the ark (using highest possible estimates, and taxonomic figures provided by evolutionists), and showed that the biblical account **can** fit known scientific facts regarding these matters (1961, pp. 65-69). Some, however, have suggested that such efforts are little more than "mental gymnastics" (Clayton, 1980, p. 8). This we categorically deny. It is not "mental gymnastics" to examine the physical structure and size of the ark **given by the Bible itself**, as compared to **known scientific facts** regarding the animal creation. In fact, rather than being mental gymnastics, it serves to show the fallacious nature of the arguments set forth by those who would criticize the inspired accounts.

Some, like Custance, have either stated or implied that the building of such a large boat as the ark, in such remote times of antiquity and by so few men, was simply not possible, or at best highly unlikely. Regarding such statements, we offer these comments. First, as Whitcomb and Morris have noted:

> The Scriptures, however, do not suggest that Noah and his three sons had to construct the Ark without the help of hired men. Nevertheless, we agree that the sheer massiveness of the Ark staggers the imagination. In fact, this is the very point of our argument: for Noah to have built a vessel of such magnitude simply for the purpose of escaping a local flood is inconceivable. The very size of the Ark should effectively eliminate the local-Flood view from serious consideration among those who take the Book of Genesis at face value (1961, p. 11).

Second, as Filby has commented:

> Yet even granting all this some may feel that the Ark was too large for early man to have attempted. A survey of the ancient world shows in fact the very reverse. One is constantly amazed at the enormous tasks which our ancestors attempted. The Great Pyramid was not the work of the later Pharaohs; it was the work of the 4th Dynasty— long before Abraham! This pyramid contained over two million blocks of stone each weighing about 2½ tons. Its vast sides, 756 feet long, are set to the points of the compass to an accuracy of a small fraction of one degree! The so-called Colossi of Memnon again are not of recent times—they belong to the 18th Dynasty of Egypt. Cut from blocks of sandstone they weigh 400 tons each and were brought 600 miles to their present position.... As our thoughts go back to the Colossus of Rhodes, the Pharos Lighthouse, the Hanging Gardens, the Ziggurats, the Step Pyramid—or even in our own land, to Stonehenge—we have no reason to suppose that early man was afraid to tackle great tasks (1970, p. 92).

Custance's argument is thus shown to be completely at odds with historical data. Merely because the ark was large does not mean the task was impossible. And we must not forget that Noah had 120 years in which to build the ark (Genesis 6:3).

The Gathering, Storage, and Care of the Animals

Objections of every kind have been raised regarding the Genesis record of the Flood, but perhaps none has been so loudly echoed as those relating to the gathering, storage, and care of the animals once they were placed into the ark. As early as 1854, John Pye Smith began raising objections (1854, p. 145), and local flood advocates have been raising them ever since. Basically, objections can be grouped under four main headings: (1) gathering of the animals; (2) storage of the animals; (3) care of the animals; and (4) migration of the animals after the Flood.

The objection has been raised that it would be impossible for creatures from different regions of the world to leave their respective homes and meet Noah in the Mesopotamian Valley. The unique creatures of Australia, for example, certainly could not have traveled to the ark, since Australia is separated by an ocean. And how could the polar bear survive a journey from his native land to the sultry plains of Mesopotamia? The variety of climates, the difficult geography, and other various and asundry items would seemingly make such journeys impossible. Some have viewed these "impossible journeys" as militating against the accuracy of the Flood account. Whitcomb and Morris, in commenting on such arguments, observed:

> An equally serious fault in this type of reasoning is that it begs the question of the extent and effects of the Deluge. It assumes, for example, that climatic zones were exactly the same before the Flood as they are now, that animals inhabited the same areas of the world as they do now, and that the geography and topography of the earth continued unchanged. But on the assumptions of a universal Deluge, all these conditions would have been profoundly altered. Arctic and desert zones may never have existed before the Flood; nor the great intercontinental barriers of high mountain ranges, impenetrable jungles, and open seas (as between Australia and Southeast Asia, and between Siberia and Alaska). On this basis, it is quite probable that animals were more widely distributed than now, with representatives of each created kind of land animal living in that part of the earth where Noah was building the Ark (1961, pp. 64-65).

Rehwinkel has suggested that during the probationary period, "migration of these animals which God had intended to save might have extended over several generations of animals" (1951, p. 75). Thus, when the ark was ready for its occupants, the animals were already in the nearby geographical regions. We might also point out that Genesis 6:19-20 makes it clear that God caused the animals to "come unto Noah." Noah did not have to "go after" all the various animals. Even Bernard Ramm has admitted that the animals must have come to Noah as they were "prompted by divine instinct" (1954, p. 169). Here is an interesting point: the same "power" that brought the animals to Adam to be named (Genesis 2:19) also brought them to Noah to be saved from the Flood. If not, why not?

After acknowledging the gathering of the animals into the ark by God's intervention, how do we explain the storage and care of the animals once in the ark? We have already examined the size of the ark. Genesis 6:14 states that Noah was to build "rooms" (cubicles, cells, or cabins) in the ark to hold the animals. Once onboard, the animals were put into these "rooms" for the long trip. We need to remember, of course, that the Genesis "kind" (Hebrew, *min*) is not the same as the biologist's "species" of today. Noah did not have to take two or seven of every **species** of animal. He had to take two (or seven) of every "kind." That there was ample room on the ark for all these animals has already been discussed, both here and elsewhere (cf. Whitcomb and Morris, 1961, pp. 65-69).

But critics are still plagued with what they think are insurmountable problems. How could eight people possibly feed and care for all the different animals on the ark? Ramm, as one such critic, complained: "The problem of feeding and caring for them would be enormous. The task of carrying away manure and bringing food would completely overtax the few people in the ark." He further suggested that the problem of "special diets and special conditions needed for the animals overthrows the idea of a universal flood" (1954, p. 167).

Apparently, Ramm has overlooked several important factors. First, of course, is the fact that his local flood theory suffers from the exact same problem. Even if the Flood were local, the care and feeding of the animals would **still** present a major problem. Second, if the animals could have been "prompted by divine instinct" (to use Ramm's own words) to come to the ark, could they not be taken care of once in the ark by He Who is responsible for that "divine instinct"?

Third, Ramm has overlooked two important Bible passages. Genesis 7:1 records, "And Jehovah said unto Noah, **Come** thou and all thy house into the ark..." (emp. added). Reading the verse from a version of the Bible that has it translated correctly (KJV, ASV), one sees God instructing Noah not to "go over there and get in that ark," but rather to "**Come** into the ark"—a personal invitation from the Creator and Sustainer of the Universe to join Him on a year-long trip! The point is: **God was with Noah and his family**. This is depicted quite graphically in Genesis 8:1 where it is stated that God "remembered" Noah and all the animals in the ark. The Hebrew word *zakar,* translated "remembered," suggests God's continued watch over the occupants of the ark. In the Scriptures, God's "remembering" always implies His movement toward the object of His memory (cf. Genesis 19:29; Exodus 2:24; Luke 1:54-55, et al.). In fact, the primary meaning of *zakar*, according to Hebrew usage, is "granting requests, protecting, delivering" when God is the subject and persons are the object (Brown, Driver, Briggs, 1979, p. 270).

Noah and his family were not left "on their own" to tackle this giant task. God was "with them" and "remembered them." The **how** of this process is not specifically stated in the inspired text. Whitcomb has suggested that possibly God supernaturally imposed a year-long "hibernation process" on the animals, thereby minimizing the necessity of a great deal of food and care.

> What Biblical evidence do we find to support this significant concept? **First**, we must assume that God supernaturally controlled the bodily functions of these animals to bring them to the Ark in the first place, overcoming all of their natural instincts during that period of time. All alternative possibilities have been shown to be hopelessly inadequate. **Second**, there could have been no multiplication of animals (not even the rabbits) during the year of the Flood, for the Ark was built just large enough to carry two of each, and the animals entered the Ark two by two and a year later went out of the Ark two by two. Note that

it was not until **after** Noah brought the creatures out of the Ark that God commanded them to "breed abundantly in the earth, and be fruitful, and multiply upon the earth" (8:17).... In the entire matter of gathering the animals to the Ark and caring for them during the year of the Flood, the Book of Genesis is **consistently supernatural** in its presentation (1973, p. 32, emp. in orig.).

While it is impossible to assert dogmatically exactly what God did in regard to gathering and caring for the animals prior to, and during, their journey, it is clear that, to use the words of Robert Jamieson, "They must have been prompted by an overruling Divine direction, as it is impossible, on any other principles, to account for their going in **pairs**" (1948, p. 95, emp. in orig.). There was some divine "overruling" in the storage, feeding, and care of the animals, to be sure. How much the Bible does not say. However, as Rehwinkel has observed:

> But, if we are willing to accept the possibility of the miraculous, some such solution is at least conceivable. The Flood as a whole was a stupendous, miraculous interference with the laws governing the entire universe; a temporary suspension of the laws governing the routine and habits of a select group of animals for one year is but an insignificant detail in comparison. The Biblical account of the Flood is so brief, and our knowledge of the world before the Flood, and particularly of the ark, is so limited that here, as elsewhere, many questions must remain unanswered (1951, p. 76).

How the animals became so widely distributed over the Earth, once they disembarked from the ark after the Flood, is not explained in the Genesis account. Whitcomb and Morris have made some very viable suggestions in *The Genesis Flood* (1961, pp. 79-86). Migrations may well have taken place by land bridges, by air, or even by direct supernatural intervention of God Himself. Other possibilities exist. For example, perhaps after the Flood those animals which came off the ark lived in or around the mountains of Ararat, and there they were able to "breed abundantly in the earth, and multiply upon the earth"

(Genesis 8:17). Their **descendants** then migrated slowly, generation after generation, until the Earth was once again filled with animal life. Critics often are heard to ask questions like, "How did the unique animals like marsupials get back to Australia, for example?" [NOTE: For a discussion of this topic, see Major, 1989, 9:29-30.] There is a significant assumption in that question, however. Who can **prove** that the marsupials were in Australia **before** the Flood in the first place? Some points we do know; some we do not. We do know that a certain number of every "kind" of air-breathing animal went into the ark; representatives of each "kind" came off the ark; those that came off the ark bred and multiplied, filling the Earth once more with animal life. Exactly how they migrated (or were distributed) to various parts of the Earth, how long that took, or why some animals later became extinct, we may not be able to distinguish conclusively. These are simply questions that will have to remain unanswered.

The Depth and Duration of the Flood

Genesis 7:11 gives us some indication of the devastating nature of the Flood when it states that "all the fountains of the great deep [were] broken up, and the windows of heaven were opened." This was no gentle spring rain. We are discussing the wrath of an angry God on a sin-sick world (refer to the previous section on the reason for the Flood). Water came down ("the windows of heaven were opened") and water rose up ("all the fountains of the great deep were broken up") until finally we find, in Genesis 7:19-20, one of the most important biblical statements regarding the universal nature of the Flood: "And the waters prevailed exceedingly upon the earth; and all the high mountains that were under the whole heaven were covered. Fifteen cubits upward did the waters prevail; and the mountains were covered." The statement of Whitcomb and Morris is pertinent here: "One need not be a professional scientist to realize the tremendous implications of these Biblical statements. If only **one** (to say nothing of **all**) of the high mountains had been covered with water, the Flood would have been absolutely universal; for water must seek its own level—and must do so quickly!" (1961, pp. 1-2, emp. in orig.).

Critics, however, have been quick to point out that the phrase "all the high mountains" need not necessarily mean **all** the high mountains, for the word "all" can be used in a relative or distributive sense. H.C. Leupold has dealt a death-blow to that argument.

> A measure of the waters is now made by comparison with the only available standard for such waters—the mountains. They are said to have been "covered." Not a few merely but "all the high mountains under all the heavens." One of these expressions alone would almost necessitate the impression that the author intends to convey the idea of the absolute universality of the Flood, e.g., "all the high mountains." Yet since "all" is known to be used in a relative sense, the writer removes all possible ambiguity by adding the phrase "under all the heavens." A double "all" (*kol*) cannot allow for so relative a sense. It almost constitutes a Hebrew superlative. So we believe that the text disposes of the question of the universality of the Flood (1942, pp. 301-302).

How deep, then, was this water "over all the high mountains"? The text says it was "fifteen cubits upward" that the water "prevailed." This phrase obviously cannot mean that the waters went only fifteen cubits high (approximately 22½ feet), for the phrase is qualified by the one that immediately follows—"and the mountains were covered." The true meaning of the phrase is to be found in comparing Genesis 7:19-20 with Genesis 6:15, where it is stated that the ark was thirty cubits high. The phrase "fifteen cubits" must then refer to the draught of the ark. The draught of a boat such as the ark is generally half its height. That is, when fully loaded, it sinks in the water to a depth equal to half the height. If the ark was thirty cubits high, and sank half of that, it would sink fifteen cubits. If the waters then prevailed upward "fifteen cubits," that would be adequate to protect the ark as it floated on the waters all over the Earth for a little over a year. The ark, therefore, would not hit any mountain tops during its journey. [NOTE: Since Psalm 104:8 speaks of God "raising up new mountains after the Flood, it is likely that the mountains of Noah's day were not as high as the mountains which we see today upon the Earth. It seems probable that the mountains of the early Earth were much smaller than, say, such peaks as Mt. Everest or Mt. McKinley that are so well known to us today.]

A careful reading of the Genesis text will indicate that the Flood lasted approximately a year. By way of summary, Whitcomb and Morris have written:

> The order of events as set forth in the first part of the eighth chapter of Genesis would seem, then, to be as follows: (1) After the waters had "prevailed upon the earth" 150 days, the waters began to assuage. (2) The Ark rested upon the mountains of Ararat the same day that the waters began to assuage, for the 17th day of the 7th month was exactly 150 days after the Flood began. (3) The waters continued to subside, so that by the 1st day of the 10th month (74 days later), the tops of various lower mountains could be seen. This would suggest a drop of perhaps fifteen or twenty feet a day, at least during the initial phase of this assuaging period. (4) The Flood level continued to fall for forty more days, so that Noah, no longer fearing that the Flood would return, sent forth a raven to investigate the conditions outside the Ark (1961, p. 7).

The Testimony of the Apostle Peter

One of the most important and convincing passages relating to the magnitude and significance of the biblical Flood is found in II Peter 3:3-7:

> ...knowing this first, that in the last days mockers shall come with mockery, walking after their own lusts, and saying, Where is the promise of his coming? for, from the day that the fathers fell asleep, all things continue as they were from the beginning of the creation. For this they wilfully forget, that there were heavens from of old, and

an earth compacted out of water and amidst water, by the word of God; by which means the world that then was, being overflowed with water, perished: but the heavens that now are, and the earth, by the same word have been stored up for fire, being reserved against the day of judgment and destruction of ungodly men.

In this marvelous passage, Peter spoke of some who—because of a fatal adherence to the false doctrine of uniformitarianism—would not seriously consider the fact that Christ is indeed going to return, and that His return will be a cataclysmic, universal intervention by God into the affairs of men. These "mockers" were convinced that all things were continuing as they had "from the beginning of the creation."

However, Peter's answer to these skeptics forever destroyed their uniformitarian arguments. Peter used two events, which cannot be explained on the mere basis of uniformitarianism, to accomplish that task. The first of these events was the creation of the world: "There were heavens from of old, and an earth...by the word of God." The second of these events was the Great Flood of Noah: "The world [*kosmos*] that then was, being overflowed with water, perished." Peter used the account of the Noahic Flood to draw a comparison with Christ's second coming and subsequent destruction of the world. For, said Peter, as "the world that then was" perished by **water,** so the "heavens that now are, and the earth" have been "stored up for **fire,** being reserved against the day of judgment and destruction of ungodly men." From Peter's language, it is impossible for men to sanely state that Peter meant a coming destruction by fire of only **part** of the Earth! Peter's terms—"the heavens that **now are, and the earth**"—are obviously universal. Peter portrayed one event that brought about a transformation not just of the Earth, but also of the heavens as well. That event, according to the inspired apostle, was the Noahic Flood!

It was the Flood that constituted the line of demarcation between "the heavens from of old" and "the heavens that now are" in the thinking of the apostle Peter. It was the

Flood that utilized the vast oceans of water out of which and amidst which the ancient earth was "compacted," unto the utter destruction of the *kosmos* "that then was." It was the Flood to which Peter appealed as his final and incontrovertible answer to those who chose to remain in willful ignorance of the fact that God **had at one time** in the past demonstrated His holy wrath and omnipotence by subjecting "all things" to an overwhelming, cosmic catastrophe that was on an absolute par with the final day of judgment, in which God will yet consume the earth with fire and cause the very elements to dissolve with fervent heat (II Peter 3:10) (Whitcomb, 1973, pp. 57-58, emp. in orig.).

British scholar Derek Kidner, in his book, *Genesis: An Introduction and Commentary*, has noted correctly that

> ...we should be careful to read the [Flood—BT] account wholeheartedly in its own terms, which depict a **total** judgment on the ungodly world already set before us in Genesis—not an event of debatable dimensions in a world we may try to reconstruct. The whole living scene is blotted out, and the New Testament makes us learn from it the greater judgment that awaits not only our entire globe but the universe itself (2 Peter 3:5-7) (1967, p. 95, emp. in orig.).

An interesting question comes to mind. If the New Testament "makes us learn" from the Noahic flood account that the coming judgment of which Peter spoke so eloquently will indeed involve "not only our entire globe but the universe itself," how can this lesson be learned from a flood that was only local in extent?

There can be no doubt, then, that Peter's argument provides inspired testimony as to the universal destruction of that Flood. "Anything less than a catastrophe of such proportions would upset the entire force of the apostle's argument and would give much encouragement to those who would teach what he so solemnly condemned" (Whitcomb, 1973, p. 59).

The Testimony of Jesus Christ

In Luke 17:26-30 (cf. Matthew 24:39), the Lord made the following statements:

And as it came to pass in the days of Noah, even so shall it be also in the days of the Son of man. They ate, they drank, they married, they were given in marriage, until the day that Noah entered into the ark, and the flood came, and destroyed them **all**. Likewise even as it came to pass in the days of Lot; they ate, they drank, they bought, they sold, they planted, they builded; but in the day that Lot went out from Sodom it rained fire and brimstone from heaven, and destroyed them **all**: after the same manner shall it be in the day that the Son of man is revealed (emp. added).

The Lord thus predicted an impending doom upon the Jews of His day who would not heed the Word of God. But for our purpose here, note the context into which Jesus placed the Flood's destruction. He placed the Flood alongside the destruction of Sodom. He also placed it alongside the destruction of the ungodly at His second coming. As Whitcomb and Morris have suggested:

This fact is of tremendous significance in helping us to determine the sense in which the word "all" is used in reference to those who were destroyed by the Flood.

Our argument proceeds in the following manner: the force of Christ's warning to the ungodly concerning the doom which awaits them at the time of His Second Coming, by reminding them of the destruction of the Sodomites, would be **immeasurably weakened** if we knew that **some** of the Sodomites, after all, had escaped. This would allow hope for the ungodly that some of **them** might escape the wrath of God in that coming day of judgment. But we have, indeed, no reason for thinking that any Sodomite did escape destruction when the fire fell from heaven.

In exactly the same manner, Christ's warning to future generations, on the basis of what happened to the ungodly in the days of Noah, would have been pointless if part of the human race had escaped the judgment waters....

Therefore, we are persuaded that Christ's use of the word "all" in Luke 17:27 must be understood in the absolute sense; otherwise the analogies would collapse and the warnings would lose their force. A heavy burden of proof rests upon those who would maintain that only a part of the human race was destroyed in the Flood, in view of the clear statements of the Lord Jesus Christ (1961, pp. 21,22, emp. in orig.).

The Rainbow Covenant and Its Implications

A point that is often overlooked by local flood advocates is the rainbow covenant that God gave (Genesis 9:11-15). God promised (three times—Genesis 8:21; 9:11; 9:15) never again to destroy "everything living" and "all flesh" by a flood. He set His bow (rainbow) in the heavens as a sign of that promise. If the Flood of Genesis 6-8 was only a local flood, then it is plainly obvious that God has broken His covenant promise repeatedly, since there have been countless local floods upon the face of the Earth in which multiplied thousands of people have perished. If the Genesis Flood was local, but God promised never to send another (local) flood, then why have local floods continued? The advocates of the local flood theory have God breaking His promise, in spite of plain statements of Scripture like Titus 1:2 that state that God "cannot lie." S.J. Schultz has stated:

> Had any part of the human race survived the flood outside of Noah and his family they would not have been included in the covenant God made here. The implication seems to be that all mankind descended from Noah so that the covenant with its bow in the cloud as a reminder would be for all mankind (1955, p. 52).

To those who respect the inspiration of Scripture, the arguments that establish the Flood as a global, universal, worldwide event are incontrovertible.

6

CONCLUSION

As we have examined the biblical doctrine of the Great Flood of Genesis 6-8, we have attempted to draw conclusions based on sound, scriptural evidence and proper exegesis. For example, we noted that without the inspired testimony of both the Old and New Testaments, we would know little about the entire Flood incident. We have mentioned, and wish to repeat here for emphasis, the fact that the Scriptures **are** inspired (verbal, plenary inspiration) and that we are dependent upon them for materials relating to the Noahic Flood. We have examined the reason for the Flood—man's sin in rebelling against God. We have noted many supernatural elements relating to the Flood, without which it would have been impossible. At the same time, however, we have noted that many events connected with the Flood (the building of the ark, Flood water damage, etc.) were purely natural, not supernatural, in scope. We have observed the ubiquity of flood myths, stories, and legends. We have documented the attacks made on, and the compromises made of, the Genesis account of the Flood, and have explained, and refuted, each of these attacks and/or compromises.

Lastly, it has been our intent to explain why the Bible demands a global, universal Flood, and not merely a local inundation of some kind. By examining such factors as the need for an ark, the design and construction of the ark, the size of the ark, the gathering and care of the animals, etc., we have explained the necessity of accepting the universal nature of the Flood. And, of course, we have examined at length biblical testimony from a variety of sources regarding the Flood (Jesus, Peter, etc.).

It has not been our intent to give an in-depth examination to the many scientific evidences for a worldwide Flood. Entire volumes have been written documenting such evidences. The classic volume *The Genesis Flood*, from which we have frequently quoted, is an excellent source of such material. John Whitcomb's two books, *The World That Perished* and *The Early Earth*, are good sources for additional material. Harold Clark has also written a book dealing with such matters (*Fossils, Flood and Fire*). Other books (*The Flood*, by Rehwinkel; *Speak Through the Earthquake, Wind & Fire*, by Fisher) are readily available, and speak to the fact of the multiplicity of scientific evidences supporting the global Flood.

As we draw this study to a close, however, several comments need to be made regarding any study of the Flood, and especially scientific evidences supporting that Flood. After a thorough study of the biblical evidences for a global, universal Flood has been completed, it is appropriate to ask, "What evidences, if any, are available from scientific studies which might further assist us in our study of the Flood?" Surely, if there was a global, universal Flood of the extent of the Great Flood of Noah, some evidence must be available from science regarding such an event.

Indeed, there is evidence from science which indicates that a global catastrophe of the nature of the Genesis Flood did once occur. However, a word of caution is in order here. In the past, extremes have been evident among those who have attempted to study the scientific evidences for the Noahic Flood. We have seen such statements as: "...There is no way geologically of supporting the idea that there was a worldwide flood...." (Clayton, undated). But, on the other hand, there have been those who have taken every shred of evidence to mean that "**this** indicates a global Flood" or "**that** indicates a global Flood." Consequently, even certain layers of the Earth were once identified as "Flood layers" of such-and-such a date, only later to be discarded as evidence for a global Flood. It would be wise to avoid both extremes.

We know from biblical evidence that there was once a universal Flood. Knowing that, we may then be alert to evidences from science that might possibly be the result of such a Flood. What exactly those evidences might be is not always easy to say, for no one among us has ever seen or experienced a global Flood. Nor have we spoken with anyone who has. What measurements we are able to make now must, by necessity, be made on a much smaller scale (e.g., using local flood information, etc.). This being the case, caution is in order, for we do not want to abuse, or misuse, evidence from science in any way, even unintentionally.

Critics of what has been called "Flood geology" are quick to point out what they see as "flaws" in the system that attempts to interpret Earth history in light of the global catastrophe of Genesis 6-8. They delight in finding "problem areas" in this regard. Certainly, none among us would advocate that there are no difficulties with respect to the Flood theory of geology. Even those who are at the forefront in writing and speaking on these topics are open and honest enough to admit that they do not have all the answers. However, neither do we gain anything by insisting that attempts to interpret Earth history through the eyes of the Flood account are futile, and that we would be better off advocating uniformitarian views of Earth history, as some among us seem to be suggesting. In fact, attempts to avoid **any possible** interpretation of Earth history via Flood geology, and to harmonize interpretations of Earth history via strictly natural processes, present more problems than they solve. As professor Cockburn so well stated: "No man departs from the Flood theory upon pretense of avoiding any absurdity therein supposed, but that he ran himself upon the necessity of believing greater absurdities than any he pretended to avoid" (1750, p. 163).

While there may be some "problem areas" with coming to a full and complete scientific, after-the-fact understanding of the geology associated with Noah's Flood, the arguments for a local flood—allegedly based on the Bible or from science—are not convincing. There are, however, overwhelming arguments in favor of the universal deluge. Henry M. Morris, for example, in his work, *The Remarkable Birth of Planet Earth*, has suggested 96 arguments (64 biblical, 32 non-biblical) for a worldwide Flood (1972, pp. 96-100). And while one may not agree with every single argument set forth, it will quickly become apparent that it is impossible to dispose of each of the arguments in some kind of nonchalant or frivolous manner.

Vast animal graveyards and fossiliferous rubble shifts have been found worldwide. Evidence has been documented of a sudden, watery cataclysm, followed by a deep freeze across the entire great north, accompanied by titanic hydraulic forces and crustal upheavals, burying a host of mastodons, elephants, and other great beasts in a region that is now almost totally devoid of vegetation. Vast numbers of fossil trees and plants, standing erect, oblique and even inverted while piercing through successive beds of water-laid stone have been discovered. There is abundant evidence (as we have already documented) of profuse vegetation and a temperate, even subtropical, climate prevailing in Antarctica and the northern polar regions at some time in the past. Worldwide fossilization has occurred in vast quantities, including fossils of even many modern forms of life. These fossils are found in sedimentary strata, often at great depths and under great pressure. Vast and numerous rifts, fissures, and lava beds have been discovered, scarring the world's ocean floor, all clearly recent and bespeaking some gigantic submarine upheaval of the Earth's crust (as in the breaking up of the "fountains of the deep"). Marine fossils have been found buried and exposed at almost every altitude. Many additional evidences could be listed as well. And, while it is not our intention to suggest that **every** instance of rapid burial or mass destruction is directly attributable to the Flood, many, in fact, may well be. [NOTE: The reader who is interested in a discussion of some well-known cases of fossilization that may turn out not to be Flood-related (e.g., woolly mammoths in Arctic regions) is encouraged to examine articles by Major (1989), and Oard (1990, pp. 86-91).]

Let us openly and fairly examine such evidences, and urge others to do likewise. Let us be cautious as good students, but never willing to compromise inspired testimony. And let us remember that what is today's scientific theory may well turn out to be tomorrow's superstition. Knowing this, let us respect all the more God's unchanging, divine revelation.

REFERENCES

Arkell, W.J. (1956), *Jurassic Geology of the World* (New York: Hafner).

Bancroft, H.H. (undated), *Works: The Native Races of the Pacific Slope—Mythology*, Vol. III.

Brown, Francis, S.R. Driver, and Charles B. Briggs (1979 edition), *A Hebrew and English Lexicon of the Old Testament* (Peabody, MA: Hendrickson).

Buffaloe, Neal D. and N. Patrick Murray (1981), *Creationism and Evolution* (Little Rock, AR: The Bookmark).

Clark, Harold W. (1968), *Fossils, Flood and Fire* (Escondido, CA: Outdoor Pictures).

Clayton, John N. (1976), *The Source* (South Bend, IN: Privately published by author).

Clayton, John N. (1978), "The Question of Methuselah," *Does God Exist?*, 5[6]:11-13.

Clayton, John N. (1980), "The Flood—Fact, Theory and Fiction," *Does God Exist?*, 7[7]:2-9.

Clayton, John N. (Undated), *Questions and Answers: Number 1* [taped lecture], (South Bend, IN: Privately published by author).

Cockburn, Patrick (1750), *An Enquiry into the Truth and Certainty of the Mosaic Deluge,* as quoted in Byron C. Nelson (1968), *The Deluge Story in Stone* (Grand Rapids, MI: Baker).

Colbert, E.H. (1949), "Evolutionary Growth Rates in the Dinosaurs," *Scientific Monthly*, 69:71.

Custance, Arthur C. (1958), *The Extent of the Flood: Doorway Papers No. 41* (Ottawa, Canada: Privately published by author). This material by Custance was later included in his 1979 book, *The Flood: Local or Global?*, (Grand Rapids, MI: Zondervan).

Custance, Arthur C. (1979), *The Flood: Local or Global?* (Grand Rapids, MI: Zondervan).

Dawson, John William (1895), *The Historical Deluge in Relation to Scientific Discovery* (Chicago, IL: Revell).

Dillow, Joseph (1981), *The Waters Above* (Chicago, IL: Moody).

Epp, Theodore (1972), *The God of Creation* (Lincoln, NE: Back to the Bible).

Filby, Frederick A. (1970), *The Flood Reconsidered* (Grand Rapids, MI: Zondervan).

Fisher, Graham A. (1982), *Speak Through the Earthquake, Wind & Fire* (Merseyside, England: Countyvise, Ltd.)

Hitchcock, Edward (1854), *The Religion of Geology and Its Connected Sciences* (Boston: Phillips, Sampson, & Co.).

Jackson, Wayne (1984), "Evolution and Creation: Are They Compatible?," *Christian Bible Teacher*, 28[7]:296-297.

Jackson, Wayne and Bert Thompson (1992), *In the Shadow of Darwin: A Review of the Teachings of John N. Clayton* (Montgomery, AL: Apologetics Press).

Jamieson, Robert (1948 reprint), *Critical & Experimental Commentary*, (Grand Rapids, MI: Eerdmans).

Kearley, F. Furman (1979), "The Significance of the Genesis Flood," *Sound Doctrine*, March/April.

Kidner, Derek (1967), *Genesis: An Introduction and Commentary* (Chicago, IL: Inter-Varsity Press).

Kinns, Samuel (1886), *Moses and Geology* (London: Cassell & Co.).

Leupold, Herbert C. (1942), *Exposition of Genesis* (Columbus, OH: Wartburg Press).

Major, Trevor J. (1989), "Questions and Answers," *Reason & Revelation*, 9[8]:29-30.

Major, Trevor J. (1989), "Ice Ages and Genesis," *Reason & Revelation*, 9[11]:41-44.

Major, Trevor J. (1994), "Questions and Answers," *Reason & Revelation*, 14:[5]:39.

Montgomery, John Warwick (1972), *The Quest for Noah's Ark* (Minneapolis, MN: Bethany Fellowship).

Morris, Henry M. (1972), *The Remarkable Birth of Planet Earth* (San Diego, CA: Institute for Creation Research).

Nelson, Byron (1931), *The Deluge Story in Stone* (Minneapolis, MN: Augsburg).

Oard, Michael J. (1990), *An Ice Age Caused by the Flood* (El Cajon, CA: Institute for Creation Research).

Ramm, Bernard (1953), *Protestant Christian Evidences* (Chicago, IL: Moody).

Ramm, Bernard (1954), *The Christian View of Science and Scripture* (Grand Rapids, MI: Eerdmans).

Rehwinkel, Alfred M. (1951), *The Flood* (St. Louis, MO: Concordia).

Riem, Johannes (1925), *Die Sintflut in Sage und Wissenschaft* (Hamburg: Germany; Das Rauhe Haus), translation provided by Rehwinkel (1951, p. 129).

Rush, David E. and Larry Vardiman (1990), "Pre-Flood Vapor Canopy Radiative Temperature Profiles," *Proceedings of the Second International Conference on Creationism—1990,* ed. R.E. Walsh and C.L. Brooks (Pittsburgh, PA: Creation Science Fellowship).

Schultz, S.J. (1955), "The Unity of the Race: Genesis 1-11." *Journal of the American Scientific Affiliation*, 7:52.

Smith, John Pye (1854), *The Relation Between the Holy Scriptures and Some Parts of Geological Science* (London: Henry G. Bohn).

Thompson, Bert (1992), "The Bible, Science, and the Ages of the Patriarchs," *Reason & Revelation*, 12[5]:17-20.

Wallace, Alfred Russel (1876), *The Geographical Distribution of Animals* (New York: Harper & Brothers).

Warfield, Benjamin B. (1948), "The Real Problem of Inspiration," *The Inspiration and Authority of the Bible*, ed. Samuel C. Craig (Philadelphia, PA: Presbyterian & Reformed).

Whitcomb, John C. (1973), *The World That Perished* (Grand Rapids, MI: Baker).

Whitcomb, John C. and Henry M. Morris (1961), *The Genesis Flood* (Philadelphia, PA: Presbyterian & Reformed).

Whitelaw, Robert L. (1975), "The Testimony of Radiocarbon to the Genesis Flood," *Symposium on Creation*, ed. Donald W. Patten (Grand Rapids, MI: Baker), Vol. 5.

Willis, John (1979), *Genesis* (Austin, TX: Sweet).

Woods, Clyde (1972), *The Living Way Commentary on the Old Testament: Genesis-Exodus* (Shreveport, LA: Lambert).

Wundt, William (1916), *Elements of Folk Psychology* (New York: Macmillan). Translated by Edward L. Schaub.